Bursts of
Inspiration

WALLACE J. CASE

Messenger for the Word of God

Published 2013.

Printed in the United States of America

ISBN 978-0-9854522-0-9

OMG Press
6560 W. 46th Avenue
Wheat Ridge, CO 80033
www.omgpress.com

OMG
PRESS

CONTENTS

ACKNOWLEDGEMENT

Special thanks to my Sister, Debbie Morgen, for editing and for the encouragement of writing these poems.

I am pleased to share these bursts of inspiration with you. You know God the giver of gifts, gives them to his children so we may glorify Him through our gifts. Now these gifts vary but yet are meant for the same purpose. The list is endless. So this gift is from my heavenly Father through his Holy Spirit in the name of his Son Jesus Christ who through Him I can do all things.

I give glory to Him for these precious bursts of inspiration.

Philippians 4:13

ARMOR OF LIGHT

Be strong in the Lord and in his mighty power
Put on the full armor of God as the devil schemes to devour.
Against flesh and blood is not our battle at hand
But against rulers, authorities and powers of this darkened land.

When the time of evil comes stand firm and hold your ground
At your waist the belt of truth you must wrap around.
Put on the breast plate of righteousness as the devil will attack
    the heart
May the gospel of peace ready your feet where the Holy Spirit
    may have you start.

Take up the shield of faith for in faith God you will please
The shield will extinguish flaming arrows the evil one
    will conceive.
Wear the helmet of salvation to protect your mind from doubt
Sharpen the sword of the spirit which is the word of God
    you'll shout.

Pray in all occasions leave the darkness to the night
Pray for all the Lord's people as we wear His armor of light.

Romans 13:12/Ephesians 6:10-17

BREATH OF LIFE

God Breathed Adam's first breath of life
And then breath to Eve God gave to his wife.
Now God was the image for man he created
His word holds the truth when it is debated.

New breath of life is breathed every day
Existing breath come what may.
By God's grace we have life's breath
From our Lord Jesus no sting of death.

All breath from this world whether future or past
Is given by God until we breathe our last.
But hope is not lost for in Him we remain
To live is Christ Jesus and to die is gain.

Genesis 2:7/1 Corinthians 15:55/Philippians 1:21

HEAVEN

I see heaven or so it seems
Are these my thoughts or God given dreams?
Do we believe the heaven we see?
Is this my creation deep within me?
God loves to show us what's in store
Just enough, but our hearts want more.

Our hearts will wait for the trumpet sound
To show God's will has abound.
Gates of pearls streets of gold
The multitudes will worship him
Both new saints and old.

Full of joy and a robust peace
A big mansion and a banquet feast.
Rivers flowing with pastures so green
Beautiful mountains their view so serene.
Tall standing trees and a sky so blue
I pause to think, this dream will come true.

I thank you Father for this dream
This thought of heaven of how it will seem.

Revelations 21:21

A WALK THROUGH THE BIBLE

Abba, Father it's me
May I sit upon your knee?
Tell me the story of your rising son
The fall of man or when time had begun.

Tell me of Noah and the great ark
The journey of Abraham in which he embarked,
Maybe of David and the giant he slew
The thousands you fed with fish just a few.

How about your prophets of old
Your words that they spoke so strong and so bold,
Tell me of Moses who was leading the pack
With pharaoh behind ready to attack,
The Red sea had parted your chosen had crossed
Water came crashing pharaoh had lost.

¡But my eyes grow tired; I'll miss something I fear!
Go and rest my child for tomorrow I'll be here.

1 Samuel 17:50
Matthew 14:21
Exodus 15:4

JUST TO HEAR YOUR VOICE

I lay awake at night and pray or read your word
Hoping the next sound I hear is voice I've never heard
I have heard it in my heart I have heard it in my mind
But my ears have never heard your voice
So gentle loving and kind.

When I'm feeling lonely, and I ask you if you care
Truly in my heart I really know you're there.
In this Christian life which is of my total choice
I know I'll get my chance just to hear your voice.

John 5:28/Isaiah 30:21

GOD'S WILL

God's will at times is hard to understand
Then so easy as if he takes me hand in hand.
As we walk through the valley of the shadow
Of death there are no fears.
God almighty wipes away those tears.

Within God's will there is a mighty power
That crushes evil as it tries to devour.
As we assemble Sunday, for God's will to be heard
Remember; to know God's will you must
Always read His word.

1 Peter 3:17
Psalm 23:4

FISHERS OF MEN

Cast your net on the right side
For your faith in me must abide.
Where I send you must go
and tell of my Father to and fro.

Speak only the truth tell no lies
It will fill their hearts and open their eyes.
Your flesh you will battle everyday
So call out to your Father and pray.

Persevere and endure to no end
For you have been chosen as fishers of men.

Matthew 4:19
John 21:6

THE CREATOR

God the creator of all things
Land, sea and living beings.
Green valley's where deer shall rest
Tall pines so birds can nest.

Mountains where rivers flow
Their tranquil beauty always show.
Grassy meadows, flowers of the field
With the splendor that they yield.

The heavens, earth, and the sun
With these things creation had begun.
To your eyes creation will appear
To your ears you will hear.

Praise; glory for the foundation he laid
For this is good what God has made

Gen 2:1-2

GOD'S LITTLE LAMB

God sent a little lamb
Whose heart was pure as snow.
And everywhere that lamb went
God's children were sure to go.

But evil was our problem
God knew this from the start.
So the purpose of the lamb
Was to purify our heart...

God sent this little lamb
With power and his love...
This lamb we call Jesus,
Who came down from above,
Is watching you right now
With joy and much delight,
As you lift your hands in worship;
And pray to him every night

John 1:29

PURITY

A purity no match to find
As we search within our heart and mind.
Our soul we search to no avail
We look to the world to prevail.

With hardened hearts there is no hope
In a fallen world were left to cope.
Until one day we see this light
Of purity and great might.

A robust peace we can't explain
With a love that we shall gain.
We lift our hands up to the sky
To praise this purity on high.

With his grace and much prayer
This purity claims our despair.

James 3:17

BE STILL

When the road is rugged and looks all up hill
Worry not my child be still.
When the burden of loneliness makes its stand
Be still my child take my hand.

When flaming darts come your way
Be still my child and pray.
When your eyes are not fixed and looking upright
Be still I will focus your sight.

When the enemy comes to destroy
Be still receive my joy.
Understand these words are no façade
Be still and know that I am God.

Psalm 46:10

THE THRONE ROOM

A place of pure repentance and holy praise
With down cast face or joyous gaze.
We wait to hear from our Lord
Expecting sentence from a two edged sword.

Our body shakes we start to tremble
Angels singing begin to assemble.
Christ our Lord he does appear
And whispers softly in your ear.

Do I seek judgment against you?
For the sins that you do!
Do you know where you are?
Or what brought you here from afar.

A repentant heart and purity
No other ways stand before me.
Now go my child and feel my peace
And know this joy will never cease.

Matthew 5:8/2 Corinthians 7:10

PRAYER

To commune with God we must pray
We should call unto him every day.
In the night and in the morn
To praise his name and to adorn.

We pray for joy within our heart
And your peace does not depart.
We pray for love and happiness
And for sins we must confess.

We pray for such as daily bread
To thank you for counting every hair on our head
We pray for family and our friends
For broken relations to make amends.

We pray for others eternal life
And the removal of pain and strife.
My biggest praise within these prayers
Is to know you hear me anywhere.

Romans 12:12
Philippians 4:6
James 5:16

THE DELIVERER

This cry of freedom that I hear
Ever so softly yet so near.
So I sit bound and chained
To this bondage I will remain.

My hope is lost; the pain is to great
For within my heart I met my fate.
At that moment when all is a loss
I had a vision of a man on a cross.

Can this vision be for real?
Will he deliver me from this ordeal?
In an instant I start to hear
Words of freedom ever so clear.

Forgive me Lord of my sins tonight
Fill me with your power and might.
I felt warm oil poured upon me
As broken chains set me free.

Now the freedom that I feel
Is to know eternal life is so real.

Romans 11:26
John 8:36

JOY

Painful tears fill my eyes
As satan fills our head with lies.
Do not listen or receive
As he uses these lies to deceive.

We are a children of a higher power,
Our mighty God will devour.
And joyful tears will fill our eyes
As we lift our heads up to the sky.

No greater joy can be found
Than to know your spirit is heaven bound.

John 16:20

THE GREAT I AM

Prayer and trust we must do
For God's gift has come true.

A child is born in Bethlehem
To Mary and Joseph the great I Am
He did great wonders, the Bible has said
He healed the sick he raised the dead.

All these wonders so many saw
He poured his heart out he gave his all.
He lived a life that we must live;
This great I Am has much to give.

He bore our shame; he bore our pain
His act of love was not in vain.
On the cross our Christ did die
For the sins of both you and I.

To this day his word holds true;
Remain in me and I will remain in you.
I thank you father up above,
For the gift of I Am that you sent with love.

Isaiah 43:12
Exodus 3:14

THE GREAT COMMISSION

Something great this way comes
I speak not jewels or monetary sums.
A mighty power that you will receive
First you must confess with your mouth and in your
heart believe.

Accept Jesus as your savior and king put aside every
worldly thing.
There is only one way that much is true
Christ our Lord is the door to go through.

The Lord will come Knocking, open the door it is your heart
he will restore.
When you are ready and all healed up
The Lord will send you out with a filled cup.

So do not fear worldly superstition
But share the love of Jesus and the great commission.

Mark 16:15
Acts 16:10

CONSUMING FIRE

A fire burns all in its way
But there will be a time, there will come a day...
A consuming fire that shall surge,
Within your heart, it will emerge—

A fire so strong and so intense,
Words cannot explain how big and immense.
This consuming fire burns all in its path
Is this God's love or his wrath?

So, God's children receive his love;
And let his fire consume you from above.

Deuteronomy 4:24

THE POTTER

Lord is my potter, I humbly pray
With the gentle touch of your hands, and from formless clay.
Make and shape me on your potter's wheel
Forming and strengthening through every ordeal.

May it be you I pray they will see!
So gentle and loving the vessel I'll be.
What type of vessel will you make of me?
Covered with gems for all to see?

This pride that you speak is not your purpose by far!
But you were created to be a serving jar.
When your service is over and you've been called unto
    my throne
I shall cover you with gems for it was my service you have
shown.

Isaiah 64:8

HOLY TRINITY

God the father up above
Who is just in wrath as in love…
And a Son whose life he'd give
So many other souls would live…

The Holy Spirit who convicts and anoints,
Also counsels and appoints…
You see the name of this awesome three
Is called the Holy trinity.

Their power so great, this royal host---
The Father, his Son, and the Holy Ghost.

Matthew 3:16-17

HIS TIME

When it is his time you will know
There is a time to reap and a time to sow.
There is a time to laugh and a time to cry
There is a time to live and a time to die.

There is a time for glory and a time for pain
There is a time to leave and a time to remain.
There is a time to speak and a time to hear
There is a time he seems far and a time he's near.

There is a time for silence and a time to rejoice
There is time to be still and a time to lift up your voice.
I do not know this reason or rhyme,
But I know it is within His time.

Ecclesiastes 3:1

POUR OUT YOUR SPIRIT

Pour out your Spirit let us feel your glory,
Fill our hearts with truth so we may tell your story.
As you send us out we travel to the highest peak,
And with an overflowing heart our mouths will truthfully speak.

To tell of your love and mercy to which there is no end,
And of broken hearts with your touch you mend.
Through your Holy Spirit We will make a righteous stand,
Also knowing the evil one cannot pluck us from your hand.

We pray for the pouring of your Spirit On your created land,
For we believe these promises have been since time began.

Joel 2:28
Luke 6:45
John 10:29

THE SPRING OF LIFE

This spring of life has no measure
Within this spring holds many of treasure.
Not of silver nor of gold
But a glory we seek to behold.

From God's throne this spring does flow
And water's his children's lives for their spirits to grow.
Eternal life this spring does give
By God's grace we will live.

Quench your thirst like never before
Drink from his spring and thirst no more.

John 4:10
John 4:14

THE VINE

A peace within that's so divine
The source you know is called the vine.
This vine that grows is for us
A gift from God that we must trust.

The gardener that tends the vine
Prune's the branches that entwine.
For one day that branch will bloom,
And produce the harvest he will consume.

In the twinkle of an eye,
We will meet him in the sky.
He'll hold us tight he'll hold us near
As he wipes away our every tear.

Receive these words with much love,
That is how they came from above.

John 15:1
John 15:5

GIVER OF GIFTS

The giver of gifts sometimes goes unseen
His children know the way and the means.
Some can dance, some can sing,
Some can draw anything.

Some can write, some can teach
Some are gifted to preach,
Some make you laugh, some help you talk,
Some encourage you to stay in your walk.

But the greatest gift of all
Is love, with this gift there is no law.
Spread this love to and fro,
And glory be to the giver of love he does bestow.

I have not mentioned this giver's name
It is no secret or a game.
But God almighty is of course
The giver of gift's and our life source.

Romans 12:6

FRUIT OF THE SPIRIT

Sweet nectar this fruit can be
Share it with others so they may see.
Bite right in and you will find
That this fruit is so divine.

This fruit of the Spirit is nothing new
A loving gift from God to you.
In this fruit there are many tastes
So pray for fruit without haste.

Love and joy are just a start
Peace and patience to warm the heart.
Kindness and goodness we must share
So be faithful and gentle beyond compare.

Self-control shall be shown
For by these fruit you will be known.

Galatians 5:22-23

GARDEN OF PRAYER

The garden of gethsemane
Where Jesus would go to pray
To commune with his Holy Father
For hours he would stay.

He would speak of many things
But his last in gethsemane
If he was to give up the ghost
On the cross on Calvary.

There was another garden
It was a place of peace
Where Adam could walk with God
And his presence would never cease.

We also have this garden this solemn quite space
Where we find the will of God and our troubles he'll displace
So go and rest your heart in this spiritual garden of prayer
Knowing that God will always walk with you there.

Matthew 6:6/Matthew 26:36, 42/Mark 14:32-39
Luke 22:39-46/Genesis 3:8-9

HOLY MOUNTAIN

Praise and glory to God for you are worthy to be praised,
As we gather at your holy mountain our hearts and arms we raise.
Remove thy sandals; lay your burdens down,
For where you are standing is God's holy ground.

So come let us go where Moses would learn,
From the great I Am, in a flaming bush that would not burn.
God's children he would lead and his laws that they should heed,
To a land of milk and honey where his promises would succeed.

A top this holy mountain a foundation has been laid,
The cornerstone our Christ with his love that he displayed.
This sacrificial lamb gave his life for thee,
Se we may live with him throughout eternity.

And from throughout the land all the nations they will see,
The mountain of the Lord the holy mountain it will be.

Psalm 48:1 / Micah 4:2 / Exodus 3:2-5
Isaiah 11:9 / Matthew 27:50

PROMISED LAND

The beginning of time a promise was made,
To a nation not born, still a debt to be paid.
A wandering nation Israel by name
In search of this land that they would proclaim.

It was many a year and battles were won
With God's mighty hand yet the chosen weren't done.
They laid down their swords their bows and their shields
And God gave them their towns and homes and fields.

By God's grace his promise did show
They raised up their families this nation did grow.
On earth as in heaven with God's creative hand
He led his chosen people to his promised land.

Genesis 12:1-3/Exodus 3:17/Numbers 32:13/Joshua 11:18
Joshua 24:13

AT THE FEET OF JESUS

At the feet of Jesus our crowns we lay
We will worship him with angels and saints
This day come soon I pray.

From the footstool we worship in your dwelling place
Before at the ark of your might
Now at the throne room of grace.
O' ancient of days arise our Lord come to your place of rest
We come as a body of one at your sovereign behest.

Prophesy was foretold from your Apostles of old
At the feet of Jesus we'll lay down our crowns of gold.

Revelations 4:10
Psalm 132

A KNEELING HEART

On bended knee my heart I give
By mouth profess my savior lives.
My kneeling heart you now posses
To instruct and command I do confess.

This kneeling heart the Lord holds dear
What we see in body God see's here.
A kneeling heart is not work or a chore
But a style of life we come to adore.

A kneeling heart sounds like a simple task
With the strength of Jesus you will accomplish all he will ask
The kneeling hearts key I will not hide
Your faith remains in Jesus and in his word you must abide.

Romans 10:10
Philippians 4:13
John 15:14

I JUST CALL IT HOME

We are a stranger in a foreign land
Make no mistake that was God's plan.
A land so far and a place so grand
With God and our king at his right hand.

We miss this paradise that we've not seen
Waiting for his presence this view so serene.
Our home so far away
For many a year and many a day.

The call from heaven we wait to hear
A trumpet call so loud and clear.
And the saints gather from where they roam
To some heaven or paradise, I just call it home.

Luke 23:43
Psalms 119:19
1 Thessalonians 4:16

THE CATTLE ON A THOUSAND HILLS

Psalm Asaph a word from the Lord
A musician of David speaking God's spiritual sword.

All is God's no sacrifice is just
For he made all, from heaven to earths dust
We watch over his flock and tend to his herd
We eat from his crop and share the blessing of his word.

May your faith hold true, God knows the heart
In time of testing his love will not depart.
Come near to Jesus and the devil will flee
For all belong to God including you and me.

I praise you Lord for the Son your promise fulfills
For you also own the cattle on a thousand hills.

1 Chronicles 16:4-6
Ephesians 6:17
Psalms 50

IT IS WELL

Is it well with your life's role?
It is well within my body and soul!
Oh Lord examine my heart and mind
Wash me cleanse me if sin you find.

I wash myself from head to feet
Only the blood of Jesus makes you complete.
Let Jesus wash you and in your spirit see
Unless I wash you, you have no part with me.

For it is written and Peter said
Wash not only my feet Lord, but my hands and head.
For the living water that you shall receive
It is well within your soul as you believe.

2 Kings 4:26/John 13:8-10

THE LORD IS MY STRENGTH

The joy of the Lord is my strength
For my hope is in the Lord
Light my path in darkness
And equip me with your sword.

Deliver me from evil
Which is lurking at my door
As I walk along this valley
I am alone no more.

You give strength to the weary
And increase power to the weak
We will soar on wings like eagles
To the safety of your highest peak.

We will run and not grow weary
We will walk and not faint
A new name you will give us
For your embattled saints.

We call upon your mercy within your time and length
To wait upon the Lord to receive your power and strength.

Isaiah 40:29-31/Psalm 146:5/Nehemiah 8:10

AFTERWORD

Bursts of Inspiration was inspired from times in prayer and quiet time with the Lord, words that the Lord laid on my heart that I put on paper. I recognize it as a gift from God, now to be shared with others, to bless others just as they have blessed me.

Romans 12:6 says (we have different gifts, according to the grace given to each of us. If your gift is prophesying, then prophesy in accordance with your faith.)

May these poems bless you!

www.ingramcontent.com/pod-product-compliance
Lightning Source LLC
Chambersburg PA
CBHW060633030426
42337CB00018B/3345